Joseph's Journey
Volume 6

There's a Poem for That

Joseph's Journey
Volume 6

There's a Poem for That

by

Joseph Fram

Everlasting Publishing
Vancouver, Washington
USA

Joseph's Journey
Volume 6

There's a Poem for That

by
Joseph Fram

Library of Congress Control Number
2009909828

ISBN: 0-9824844-6-1
ISBN-13: 978-0-9824844-6-3

First Edition
Everlasting Publishing
P.O. Box 965
Vancouver, WA 98666-0965

"There's a Poem for That" is dedicated to all my friends and/or strangers who provided me with a catch phrase or other inspiration for each poem. It is my blessing that wherever I am, I think in poetry. I even think that God needed a court jester and He chose me.

To all those who have helped me fulfill that role, and to my daughter Dana Pride who has led me to publish – I give my grateful Thank You.

JOSEPH FRAM

Table of Contents

THERE'S A POEM FOR THAT
by
Joseph Fram

I MOSTLY SIT AROUND
PULL POEMS FROM A HAT
NO MATTER WHAT YOU'RE THINKING
I HAVE A POEM FOR THAT

IT ISN'T THAT I KNOW SO MUCH
IT'S JUST I'VE LIVED SO LONG
NOT WRITING WHAT COMES TO ME
FOR ME WOULD BE SO WRONG

I REALLY DON'T HAVE TO SEARCH
FOR A POEM TO COME TO MIND
NATURE AND MY FELLOW MAN
ARE FRUITFUL AND SO KIND

I WRITE POETRY ABOUT ANYTHING
EVEN THINGS THAT ARE NOT THERE
GOD HAS BLESSED THE WORLD
HE'S LEFT HIS POETRY EVERYWHERE

I WRITE A POEM FOR THIS AND THAT
SOMETIMES PEOPLE THAT I MEET
THEY COME TO ME AT ANYTIME
WHEN AT HOME OR ON THE STREET

FEELING FREE
by
Joseph Fram

HAVE YOU EVER FELT REALLY FREE
WHEN THERE IS NOTHING YOU MUST DO
WHEN ALL THE WORLD IS SOMEWHERE ELSE
AND THERE IS ONLY YOU

I CAN'T BEGIN TO TELL YOU
HOW GREAT IT IS TO FEEL THAT WAY
WHEN EVERYTHING IS NEW TO YOU
YOU LOOK FORWARD TO EACH DAY

I HAD A CHANCE TO DO THAT ONCE
WHEN IN ALASKA IN MY PRIME
ALL I HAD WAS A DUFFLE BAG
AND LOTS AND LOTS OF TIME

I DID NOT HEAR ANY NEWS
READ ANY PAPERS WHILE I WAS THERE
JUST MET WITH THOSE AROUND
AND THEY SEEMED TO CARE

ALL ALONE WAS REALLY NICE
WITH NO BURDENS ON MY MIND
YOU DO NOT NEED WORLDLY THINGS
WITH FEELING FREE YOU'LL FIND

FIRST THINGS FIRST

by
Joseph Fram

HAVE YOU EVER NOTICED
HOW SOME PEOPLE ARE UNKIND
YOU CAN SEE IT THEIR ACTION
DON'T KNOW WHAT'S IN THEIR MIND

I WAS BOWLING IN A LEAGUE
WHEN A HEART ATTACK KILLED A MAN
CALL A SUB THEN 911
WAS THEIR CAPTAIN'S PLAN

THEN I TOLD A FAMILY
YOU PARENT IS MIGHTY ILL
THEY DIDN'T ASK ABOUT HER
BUT THEY DID ABOUT HER WILL

THEN I SAW AN ACCIDENT
BLOOD SPILLED EVERYWHERE
O! MY GOSH THE CARPET
WAS THE OWNER'S CARE

YOU REALLY GET TO KNOW SOMEONE
WHEN IN A PANIC THEY SHOULD BURST
BY LOOKING AT WHAT THEY DO
AND PUTTING FIRST THINGS FIRST

MY LITTLE RAY OF SUNSHINE
by
Joseph Fram

DAUGHTERS ARE A JOY TO HAVE
THIS I HAVE LONG KNOWN
BUT IT IS ESPECIALLY NICE
WHEN THEY HAVE ONE OF THEIR OWN

GRANDDAUGHTERS ARE THE SPARK
THAT KEEP GRANDPARENTS ALIVE
BY WATCHING THEM GROW AND LEARN
AND HELP THE FAMILY THRIVE

YOU BRING ME SUCH NICE MEMORIES
WHEN I HELD YOU IN MY ARMS
THERE COULDN'T HAVE BEEN MORE LOVE
YOU GATHERED WITH YOUR CHARMS

THEN MY LITTLE RAY OF SUNSHINE
TURNED INTO MY LITTLE JOLLYWAG
WITH ALL YOUR ART AND TALENT
HOW COULD I HELP BUT BRAG

NOW YOU ARE ALL GROWN UP
YOU GOT YOUR COLLEGE DEGREE
I DARE YOU TO GO OUT AND FIND
A GRANDPA MORE PROUD THAN ME

GROWING UP CATHOLIC
by
Joseph Fram

GROWING UP CATHOLIC
AN EXPERIENCE I DON'T REGRET
OH, YES I HAD SOME QUESTIONS
SOME STILL LINGER YET

BUT I ENJOYED MY CHILDHOOD
HAD FAITH AND MOSTLY FUN
WHEN I GOT IN TROUBLE
I COULD TURN TO A NUN

THEY DID RAP MY KNUCKLES
WHEN IN CLASS I WENT WILD
THEY ALWAYS WOULD RECONCILE
FOR THEY KNEW I WAS A CHILD

THEY TAUGHT ME A LOT OF THINGS
THAT I USE TO THIS DAY
LOVE AND RESPECT FOR FELLOW MAN
AND WHAT WAS JESUS' WAY

I WOULDN'T TRADE MY EXPERIENCE
I LEARNED HOW KIND NUNS CAN BE
THERE WERE TIMES FOR TOUGH LOVE
I ALWAYS KNEW THEY CARED FOR ME

HOW DID I GET HERE
by
Joseph Fram

I WENT TO SEE THE DOCTOR
ANNUAL CHECKUP THAT'S ROUTINE
I'VE BEEN FEELING FINE
JUST WANT MY RECORD CLEAN

THEN HE LOOKED ME UP AND DOWN
GAVE ME TESTS TO SEE
IF EVERYTHING INSIDE
WAS THE WAY THAT IT SHOULD BE

WELL, "I'VE FOUND SOME THINGS
THAT MAYBE WE SHOULD CHANGE
YOUR EATING HABITS AND EXERCISE"
I THOUGHT THAT IT WAS STRANGE

HE TOLD ME IF I DIDN'T
I WON'T LIVE VERY LONG
I'VE LIVED SINCE THE DEPRESSION
BUT I MUST HAVE DONE IT WRONG

THEN I HAD TO ASK HIM
IN MY MIND TO MAKE IT CLEAR
IF WHAT I WAS DOING WASN'T RIGHT
THEN HOW DID I GET HERE

I'LL WRITE YOU ONE

by
Joseph Fram

A FELLOW I KNOW
QUESTIONED A POEM I WROTE
"THERE'S A POEM FOR THAT"
HE SAID AND I QUOTE

HE WAS LOOKING FOR A SUBJECT
HE HAD ON HIS MIND
ALL THROUGH MY POEMS
THAT HE COULDN'T FIND

WE TALKED FOR A WHILE
HIS SUBJECT QUITE OBSCURE
"I HAVE YOU NOW"
HE SAID THAT'S FOR SURE

IT WAS ALL RIGHT WITH ME
THAT HE FELT THAT WAY
BUT THEN YOU MUST KNOW
I HADN'T HAD MY SAY

JUST GIVE ME YOUR SUBJECT
AND BEFORE WE ARE DONE
YOU'LL HAVE YOUR NEW POEM
CAUSE I WILL WRITE YOU ONE

LIVING WITH A SPIRIT

by
Joseph Fram

THERE ARE TIMES IN LIFE
WHEN THINGS BECOME STRANGE
THE LIFE YOU HAVE KNOWN
WILL MAKE A DRASTIC CHANGE

YOU'VE HAD A LIFE TOGETHER
THAT WAS BUILT SO LONG AGO
NOW THE PERSON WITH YOU
IS SOMEONE YOU DON'T KNOW

ILLNESS TAKES HER MIND AWAY
BUT LEAVES THE BODY THERE
THE PERSON THAT YOU LIVED WITH
CAN NOT BE FOUND ANYWHERE

THEY SAY AND DO ODD THINGS
THAT SOMETIMES HURT YOUR PRIDE
THEY NEVER MEAN TO HURT YOU
THEY'RE JUST NOT THE SAME INSIDE

YOU ARE LIVING WITH A SPIRIT
OF TIMES THAT PASSED HER BY
THAT PERSON WILL NOT RETURN
NO MATTER WHAT YOU TRY

MY BROTHER GEORGE

by
Joseph Fram

HERE'S TO MY LITTLE BROTHER
OF WHOM I'VE ALWAYS BEEN PROUD
I AM SURE YOU DIDN'T HEAR IT
I NEVER SAID IT VERY LOUD

NOW THAT YOU ARE RETIRED
FROM THE WORK YOU DID SO LONG
AS YOU LOOK BACK ON YOUR TOIL
THERE WASN'T MUCH THAT WENT SO WRONG

BECAUSE YOU VALUE FAMILY
YOU'VE BEEN LOYAL TO THE END
GOD WATCHES ALL HIS CHILDREN
HE WILL GUIDE YOU ROUND THE BEND

LIFE WILL ALWAYS BE A CHALLENGE
GETTING US FROM THERE TO HERE
AS LONG AS THERE IS PEACE INSIDE
HAPPINESS GROWS YEAR BY YEAR

THERE ARE THINGS THAT I MISSED
IN THE YEARS IN WHICH YOU GREW
ONE THING ALWAYS STAYED THE SAME
THAT'S THE CHILDHOOD LOVE WE KNEW

OLD AGE NOT AN INJURY
by
Joseph Fram

I WAS PLAYING SOFTBALL
WITH YOUNGER MEN THAN ME
I WAS THE ONLY PITCHER
COULD PLATE THE BALL YOU SEE

OH, I DID ALL RIGHT I GUESS
I'D GET A HIT OR TWO
DIDN'T HAVE TO MOVE A LOT
ON THE MOUND, NOT MUCH TO DO

WE HAD A PITCHER / MANAGER
WHO WOULD PITCH ONCE IN A WHILE
MOSTLY HE SAT IN THE DUGOUT
MUNCHING GOODIES AND SMILE

I PLAYED IN THE INFIELD
I COULD NOT THROW TOO FAR
I DID FIELD THE BALL JUST FINE
BUT WAS IN NO WAY A STAR

ONE DAY IN THE OUTFIELD
WHILE RUNNING TURNED A KNEE
I CALLED FOR AN INJURY TIME-OUT
WAS TOLD "OLD AGE IS NOT AN INJURY"

JUST SOME LOVE
by
Joseph Fram

HER AUTUMN IS APPROACHING WINTER
SHE HAS LESS AND LESS TO SAY
SHE GROWS WEARY AND SO TIRED
IT GETS HARDER DAY BY DAY

HER FRIENDS AND FAMILY COME BY
THEY TRY TO DO THEIR BEST
TO CHEER HER AND TO COMFORT
I CAN SEE SHE WANTS TO REST

THEY TRY TO GET HER TO REMEMBER
THINGS FROM SO LONG AGO
SHE SMILES, NODS AND TELLS THEM
I WISH I COULD TELL YOU SO

THEY WANT HER TO DO THINGS
HER BODY WILL NOT PERMIT
TO TAKE A WALK AND EXERCISE
WHEN SHE CAN BARELY SIT

SHE APPRECIATES THEIR VISITS
BUT CANNOT DO WHAT THEY DEMAND
ALL SHE WANTS IS JUST SOME LOVE
AND LET HER CONDITION STAND

ABSOLUTE CONTROL
by
Joseph Fram

THERE ARE THOSE AMONG US
WHO MUST HAVE ABSOLUTE CONTROL
OF EACH AND EVERY SITUATION
EVEN TRY TO REACH OUR SOUL

YOU CAN SEE IT IN THEIR EYES
IF SOMETHING IS OUT OF PLACE
AS SOON AS YOU'RE NOT LOOKING
TO CORRECT IT THEY MUST RACE

IF SOMEONE TRIES TO GO ON THEIR OWN
THEY WILL DO EVERYTHING THEY CAN
TO CONTROL THE PATH THEY'RE TAKING
AND MAKE THEM CHANGE THEIR PLAN

WHEN SOMEONE THEY ARE CLOSE TO
DOESN'T DO WHAT THEY SAY
THEY NEVER FORGET THAT MOMENT
FIGURE HOW TO MAKE THEM PAY

BUT IN THE END THEY ARE ALONE
ABSOLUTE CONTROL CAN NEVER BE
WHEN YOUR GOAL IS TOTAL CONTROL
YOU CONTROL NOTHING, DON'T YOU SEE

I'M NOT DONE TALKING YET
by
Joseph Fram

EVER TRY TO TELL A STORY
ABOUT AN ADVENTURE YOU HAD
WHEN A THIRD PARTY INTERRUPTS YOU
DOESN'T THAT MAKE YOU KINDA MAD?

OR WHEN YOU BUY SOMETHING NEW
TALKING ABOUT IT IS LOTS OF FUN
SOMEONE INTERRUPTS TO TELL YOU
HIS FRIEND JUST BOUGHT A BETTER ONE

YOU'RE TELLING ABOUT AN OPERATION
THE DOCTOR SAID YOU WON'T SURVIVE
SOMEONE HAD ONE TWICE AS BAD
IT'S A WONDER THEY ARE ALIVE

I GUESS SOME PEOPLE NEVER LISTEN
DON'T WANT OTHERS TO HAVE THEIR SAY
THEY NEVER HEAR A STORY'S END
THEY GO MERRILY ON THEIR WAY

I TRY TO KEEP MY PATIENCE
THE ONE THING THAT I REGRET
THE ONES WHO INTERRUPT ME
DON'T HEAR, "I'M NOT DONE TALKING YET"

DIDN'T SHARE

by
Joseph Fram

THERE WAS A TIME
IN MY LONG GONE PAST
WHEN I HAD DREAMS
THAT I THOUGHT WOULD LAST

THE DREAMS I BUILT
WERE FROM A FAIRY TALE
I KNEW NOT THEN
THOSE DREAMS WOULD FAIL

DREAMS BUILT WITH LOVE
THOSE YOU MUST SHARE
AND FIND SOMEONE
THAT WILL ALSO CARE

I THOUGHT I HAD FOUND
THE RIGHT ONE FOR ME
AND ALL OF HER FAULTS
I COULD NOT SEE

I CANNOT HOLD HER TO BLAME
FOR THE FAILURE IN MY SCHEMES
FOR I KNEW NOT AT THE TIME
SHE DID NOT SHARE MY DREAMS

ROSEMARY

by
Joseph Fram

ROSEMARY IS YOUR GIVEN NAME
BUT ROSIE YOU ARE TO ALL
THOUGH YOU WERE NEVER BIG
YOUR DEEDS HAVE MADE YOU TALL

MEMORIES OF YESTERDAY ARE FOND
WHEN YOU WERE IN YOUR PRIME
A GREAT AND HAPPY FAMILY
HAS BEEN YOURS A LONG, LONG TIME

NOW YOU ARE TURNING EIGHT-FIVE
IT SEEMS LIKE A SHORT WHILE
WHEN BOBBY SOX AND BIG BANDS
HAD YOU IN THE CURRENT STYLE

YOU KEPT YOUR FAMILY ALL INTACT
AND ALL ARE PROUD OF YOU
I HOPE NOW AT EIGHT-FIVE
YOU FEEL THE SAME WAY TOO

FRIENDS LIKE YOU ARE HARD TO FIND
THANK YOU FOR BEING ONE TO ME
THOUGH WE ARE PARTED MANY YEARS
THAT FRIENDSHIP I STILL SEE

NEVER UNDERSTOOD
by
Joseph Fram

THERE IS A WORLD YOU BUILT
THAT IS MADE FOR ONLY YOU
THOUGH YOU MAY TRY
THERE IS NO ROOM FOR TWO

YOU TRY TO PUT A FACE ON THINGS
SO OTHERS THINK YOU CARE
BUT DEEP INSIDE YOU'RE HIDING
WITH OTHERS YOU CANNOT SHARE

YOU SAY YOU ARE A FAMILY
YOU MUST PROTECT AT ALL COST
IF SOMEONE MENTIONS THINGS LIKE LOVE
YOU ARE AT AN IMMEDIATE LOSS

MONEY, TOYS AND TRINKETS
ARE ALL YOU CARE ABOUT
IF YOU CANNOT DOMINATE SOMEONE
I GUESS THAT LEAVES THEM OUT

YOU HAVE NEVER UNDERSTOOD
THAT LOVE IS A TIE THAT BINDS
THAT SHARING THINGS TOGETHER
IS THE HEAVEN THAT ONE FINDS

WHEN GOD ISN'T LOOKING
by
Joseph Fram

WHEN GOD ISN'T LOOKING
I THINK OF THINGS I CAN DO
I OTHERWISE WOULDN'T CONSIDER
I'LL BET YOU DO TOO

HOW TO GET EVEN
WITH THE SCOUNDREL I HATE
OR WHAT ABOUT ONE-UP
WHEN NOT LIKING MY MATE

OH, NOW I REMEMBER
FROM A LONG TIME AGO
THAT MY FRIEND HURT ME
FOR WHY, I DON'T KNOW

IF GOD ISN'T LOOKING
I CAN GET EVEN SOMEHOW
FOR PAST INSULTS AND HURTS
THAT STILL BOTHER ME NOW

THEN I REMEMBER
WHAT GOD SAID TO ME
"WHEN I AM NOT LOOKING, YOU
ARE MY EYES, YOU SEE"

ALL THE THINGS I HAVE
by
Joseph Fram

WORRY, WORRY, WORRY
IS SOMETHING I USED TO DO
IF SOMEONE GOT SOMETHING
I HAD TO HAVE ONE TOO

THERE WERE JUST SO MANY THINGS
THAT I WOULD HAVE TO BUY
I GUESS JUST TO HAVE THEM
NEVER KNEW THE REASON WHY

I FILLED UP MY HOUSE
AND ALSO MY GARAGE
WITH THINGS I WOULD NEVER USE
LIKE A TOE AND FOOT MESSAGE

THEN ONE I DAY I SAW IT
PRICE TAGS ON NEW THINGS
I NEVER EVEN USED THEM
WHERE IS PLEASURE THAT IT BRINGS

NOW I DON'T HAVE TO WORRY
ABOUT THINGS THAT ARE NOT MINE
I TAKE A LOOK AT ALL I HAVE
WITH THAT I AM JUST FINE

CHECK IT OUT
by
Joseph Fram

YOU ARE DRIVING DOWN THE HIGHWAY
THERE ARE MANY THINGS YOU SEE AND DO
YOU HAVE A MULTITUDE OF DISTRACTIONS
AND GADGETS THAT OCCUPY YOU

YOU HAVE YOUR RADIO ON FULL BLAST
YOU EAT YOUR LUNCH ON THE GO
YOU SPILL YOUR DRINK ON YOUR LAP
BUT DON'T THINK THAT IT WILL SHOW

OTHER CARS JUST CREEP ALONG
YOU CAN'T PASS THEM IF YOU TRY
THEY DON'T HAVE TO BE ANYPLACE
OURS IS NOT TO REASON WHY

THEN YOU SEE THIS OTHER CAR
COMING AT YOU FROM QUITE A WAY
THEN A BIKE RIDER ON YOUR SIDE
THERE IS NO DOUBT, HE'S THERE TO STAY

THE ONCOMING CAR, BIKE AND YOU
ALL MEET AT THE SAME TIME AND PLACE
CHECK IT OUT, YOU'LL SEE IT'S TRUE
EACH TIME THIS SITUATION YOU MUST FACE

SINNER BEFORE A SAINT
by
Joseph Fram

I RAN INTO THIS GAL I KNEW
FROM A LONG TIME AGO
TRIED TO GET REACQUAINTED
THINGS WENT JUST SO-SO

WE TALKED ABOUT THE OLD TIMES
AND ALL THE FUN WE HAD
WHAT WE DID TOGETHER
ALL THE GOOD AND BAD

THEN SHE UP AND TOLD ME
SHE HAD FOUND HERSELF A BEAU
A PERFECT GENTLEMAN IN EVERY WAY
AND HOW HE LOVED HER SO

THEY WERE GOING TO SPEND A WEEK
IN SOME SECLUDED RENDEZVOUS
IN A GREAT PLATONIC RELATIONSHIP
THAT WAS ALL THAT THEY WOULD DO

THAT ALL SOUNDED WELL AND GOOD
A PRETTY PICTURE SHE COULD PAINT
ONLY TROUBLE ME HEARING THAT
I WAS A SINNER PRIOR TO A SAINT

DOZED OFF

by
Joseph Fram

I HAVE GONE TO MEETINGS
ALL GET TOGETHER FOR A PLAN
MANY HEADS ARE BETTER
WE CAN DO IT, YES WE CAN

THEN WE TALK FOR HOURS
ONE'S ASSIGNED TO TAKE NOTES
FOR OUR PRECIOUS THOUGHTS
WE ARE HOPING TO GET QUOTES

WE ALL FELT A PART OF IT
THEN OUR WORK WAS DONE
GEE! THAT WAS A GOOD JOB
MAYBE EVEN HAD SOME FUN

THEN WE WAIT WITH BATED BREATH
TO SEE OUR MASTERPIECE IN PRINT
WHEN WE FINALLY SEE IT
OF OUR WORK THERE IS NO HINT

I GUESS I MUST HAVE DOZED OFF
WHEN THE PRINTED WORDS WERE SAID
FOR ALL MY FRIENDS AND COLLEAGUES
THIS IS THE FIRST TIME IT IS READ

HOW FRAGILE
by
Joseph Fram

HOW FRAGILE IS THE HEART
THAT TEETERS ON THE BRINK
WHEN IT DEPENDS ON OTHERS
AND WHAT THEY MUST THINK

WHEN MAN IS UNSURE ENOUGH
HE QUESTIONS ALL HE DOES
EVERY MOVE HE MAKES
STOPS TO GIVE HIM CAUSE

YET MANY GO THROUGH LIFE
AND NEVER KNOW A MOMENT'S PEACE
JUST HIDING ALL THEIR FEARS
THOSE FEELINGS NEVER CEASE

IT MAKES NO DIFFERENCE WHAT THEY DO
THAT FEEING IS THERE FROM BIRTH
THEIR ONLY PEACE IS BEING ALONE
TO QUESTION WHY THEY WERE PUT ON EARTH

FRAGILE HEARTS ARE HERE TO STAY
PLEASE CONSIDER THAT WHEN YOU MEET
THEY ARE AMONG ALL YOUR FRIENDS
AND STRANGERS IN THE STREET

I CAN BUY YOU
by
Joseph Fram

I CAN BUY YOU ANYTHING
THAT YOUR HEART MAY SEEK
BUT IT MUST BE MY WAY
YOU ARE NOT ALLOWED TO SPEAK

YOU MUST LOVE ME DEARLY
BE WITH ME ALL THE WHILE
AND NO MATTER HOW YOU FEEL
YOU MUST ALWAYS HAVE A SMILE

I WILL GIVE YOU ALL THE LOVE
THAT YOUR HEART CAN STAND
I CAN MAKE EVERYTHING YOU DO
SEEM OUTSTANDING AND GRAND

DIDN'T I DO EVERYTHING FOR YOU
THAT PUTS ME ABOVE ALL OTHERS
LET'S TRY TO KEEP ALL OTHERS OUT
EVEN FAMILY AND YOUR BROTHERS

I GUESS SHE NEVER HEARD THE PHRASE
"IF YOU LOVE THEM LET THEM GO
IF THEY LOVE YOU THEY WILL RETURN"
IS SOMETHING SHE WILL NEVER KNOW

SHOESTRING

by
Joseph Fram

ONCE WHILE REFEREEING HOCKEY
IT WAS BETWEEN TWO CANADIAN TEAMS
THERE MUST HAVE BEEN SOME FEELINGS
BEFORE THE GAME STARTED IT SEEMS

BEFORE I COULD DROP THE FIRST PUCK
I HEARD A SCUFFLE BEHIND ME
OPPOSING PLAYERS DROPPED THEIR GLOVES
WOULDN'T LET THE OTHERS BE

WELL, THEY GOT THEIR PENALTIES
AND THE GAME WENT ON
ONE TEAMS SCORED SO MANY GOALS
I THOUGHT THE GOALIE WAS GONE

THEN THEY SCORED ANOTHER GOAL
HE PROTESTED A FORWARD IN THE CREASE
I TRIED TO EXPLAIN "NOT SO"
BUT HIS COMPLAINING WOULD NOT CEASE

FINALLY I HAD HAD IT
WITH FIGHTS, AND COMPLAINTS ANEW
I SAID I COULD HANG A SHOESTRING
TO STOP MORE PUCKS THAN YOU

WHEN YOUR DREAM DIES
by
Joseph Fram

WHEN YOUR DREAM DIES
YOU ARE LEFT ALL ALONE
WHAT DWELLED IN YOUR MIND
WILL NEVER BE KNOWN

THOSE DREAMS THAT YOU HAD
WERE SO CLEAR IN YOUR MIND
BUT HOW TO PUT THEM IN PLACE
YOU NEVER COULD FIND

SO YOU TRIED OTHER THINGS
BUT NONE COULD REPLACE
YOUR CHILDHOOD DREAMS
ARE GONE WITH NO TRACE

LIFE WILL NOT BE THE SAME
NO MATTER WHAT YOU MAY DO
A SUBSTITUTE PERSON
IS LIVING A LIFE FOR YOU

FOR WHEN YOUR DREAM DIES
SOME OF YOU DIES TOO
FOR THE REST OF YOUR LIFE
NOT MUCH MATTERS TO YOU

THE TEN PIN
by
Joseph Fram

MY BALL WENT INTO THE POCKET
JUST AS NICE AS IT COULD BE
WHAT SHOULD HAVE BEEN A STRIKE
LEFT THAT DARN TEN PIN STARING AT ME

IT IS A VERY TRICKY RASCAL
WITH A SNARL AND SILLY GRIN
BUT I WILL KNOCK IT FOR A LOOP
I'LL TRY NOT TO HIT IT THIN

NOW I HAVE MY LINE UP
I KNOW JUST WHAT I'LL DO
IF I CAN HIT MY BOWLING MARKS
I'LL HIT THAT DARN PIN TOO

THERE I'VE THROWN MY BALL
I HIT MY MARKS SO BALL, "STAY"
I HAVE GOT YOU NOW MY FRIEND
OH! NO BALL, "DON'T CURVE AWAY"

ANOTHER SHOT, ANOTHER OPEN
I DON'T THINK I CAN ABIDE
I'LL NEVER GET THAT TEN PIN
I'M GOING TO RUN AWAY AND HIDE

WHEN THINGS WERE DIFFERENT

by
Joseph Fram

WHEN THINGS WERE DIFFERENT
IT SEEMS SO LONG AGO
WHEN I WAS YOUNG AND STRONG
AND ALL THINGS I DID KNOW

THERE WAS THE FUN WE HAD
DOING ALL SORTS OF THINGS
WE PLAYED ALL THE GAMES
AND OUR MIND HAD WINGS

TOMORROW WAS FAR OFF
THERE WAS NO NEED TO CONSERVE
WE COULD TAKE ALL OUR CHANCES
WE GOT WHAT WE DESERVE

THEN THINGS BECAME DIFFERENT
SOMEHOW AGE TOOK ITS TOLL
OUR MINDS WERE STILL BACK THERE
BUT OUR BODIES ARE NOT WHOLE

WHEN THINGS WERE DIFFERENT
WE DID THINGS WE CAN'T DO NOW
BUT MAYBE IN OUR MEMORIES
WE STILL THINK WE CAN SOMEHOW

POWER LUNCH

by
Joseph Fram

I HAD A CHUCKLE
WHEN I HEARD SOMEONE SAY
"I'M GOING TO A POWER LUNCH"
TOOK ME BACK TO ANOTHER DAY

POWER LUNCH WAS THE THING
WHEN I WAS YOUNG AND IN MY PRIME
BOSS WANTED TO WORK THRU LUNCH
AND STEAL AN HOUR OF MY TIME

FREE MEAL IN MY MIND
WAS MY ONLY THOUGHT
BUT WHEN I ARRIVED
IT WAS I WHO BOUGHT

THEN WE WOULD HAVE TO PAY
FOR SPEAKERS THEY BROUGHT IN
AFTER A WHILE OF THIS
MY WALLET STARTED GETTING THIN

POWER LUNCH SET ME STRAIGHT
IT CLEARED MY MIND TO SEE
MY APPETITE FOR LUNCH IS GONE
IS WHAT IT DID FOR ME

FLOWERS

by
Joseph Fram

I HAVE BEEN AROUND FLOWERS
I GUESS SINCE I WAS BORN
THEY BRING ME PEACE AND JOY
WHEN I SEE THEM IN THE MORN

I REALLY NEVER PAID ATTENTION
TO THE NAME OF ANY PLANT
SO IF YOU ASK ME WHAT IT IS
I WILL TELL YOU THAT I CAN'T

I DO KNOW HOW TO PLANT THEM
FROM A POT OR FROM A SEED
I PUT ALL THE INGREDIENTS IN
FOR EVERYTHING THEY NEED

I KNOW FLOWERS FOR OCCASIONS
LIKE A ROSE ON MOTHER'S DAY
I THINK OF ORCHIDS FOR THE PROM
NOT MUCH ELSE TO SAY

SO IF YOU SHOW ME FLOWERS
I CAN TELL YOU TRUE
ALL THE COLORS JUST BY LOOKING
ISN'T THAT WHAT ONE SHOULD DO

WHEN YOU GIVE YOUR LOVE
by
Joseph Fram

WHEN YOU GIVE YOUR LOVE
YOU ASK NOTHING IN RETURN
TOO MANY GO THROUGH LIFE
AND THIS THEY NEVER LEARN

LOVE IS LIKE A GIFT FROM GOD
MEANT TO BE SHARED BY TWO
IF LOVE IS NOT RETURNED
THEN IT IS A GIFT BY YOU

YOU GIVE YOUR LOVE SO FREELY
WITH ONLY KINDNESS IN YOUR HEART
IT IS NOT MEANT AS A BARGAIN
IT IS THEIRS TO KEEP FROM THE START

IF YOU ONLY GIVE YOUR LOVE
BECAUSE YOU THINK YOU'LL GET IT BACK
THEN IT ISN'T LOVE THAT YOU GIVE
WHEN IT IS ONE THAT YOU RETRACT

SO IF YOU CAN'T GIVE LOVE
WITHOUT ANY STRINGS ATTACHED
I AM AFRAID FOR YOU MY FRIEND
THAT YOU WILL NOT BE MATCHED

POP UP

by
Joseph Fram

I TRY TO DO SOME WORK
ON THE COMPUTER IN FRONT OF ME
JUST WHEN I GET TO THE GOOD PART
A POP UP DO I SEE

THEY ALWAYS HAVE SOME THINGS
NO ONE IN THE WORLD WOULD BUY
THEY COME UP SO MANY TIMES
IT'S ENOUGH TO MAKE YOU CRY

WHEN YOU TRY TO TYPE A PAGE
IT ASKS SOME OUTRAGEOUS THING
THE INTERRUPTION ALMOST MAKES ME
GIVE MY COMPUTER A FLING

I WONDER WHAT GREAT MIND
THOUGHT UP THIS MADDENING DEVICE
I'D LIKE TO THROTTLE THEM ONCE
THEN I WOULD LIKE TO DO IT TWICE

I GUESS YOU LEARN TO LIVE WITH THINGS
BUT WITH THE POP UP I HAVE MY DOUBT
IF THE COMPUTER WEREN'T SO INGRAINED
I WOULD SIMPLY THROW IT OUT

NECESSARIES
by
Joseph Fram

CHECK FOR ALL YOUR NECESSARIES
BEFORE ANYTHING YOU START
CAUSE SURE AS THE DAY IS LONG
YOU WILL BE MISSING A VITAL PART

CHECK IN ALL YOUR POCKETS
TO SEE IF YOU HAVE EVERYTHING
I'LL BET YOU MORE THAN ONCE
YOU FORGOT YOUR CAR KEY RING

DO YOU HAVE ALL YOUR NECESSARIES
WHEN YOU PLAN TO BOARD A PLANE
LIKE YOUR TICKET LEFT AT HOME
THAT IS GOING TO DRIVE YOU INSANE

WHEN YOU WRITE YOUR GROCERY LIST
ARE ALL THE NECESSARIES WRITTEN DOWN
SO THAT WHEN YOU GET BACK HOME
YOU WON'T HAVE TO GO BACK TO TOWN

CHECKING FOR ALL YOUR NECESSARIES
IS A HABIT YOU SHOULD MAKE
IT SAVES MUCH WEAR AND TEAR
AND SO LITTLE TIME IT WILL TAKE

ON HOLD

by
Joseph Fram

CAN I PUT YOU ON HOLD
I HEARD HER SWEETLY SAY
I KNEW RIGHT THEN AND THERE
THAT I HAD LOST THE DAY

WHEN I TRIED TO PROTEST
HER END OF THE LINE WENT DEAD
MY FIRST THOUGHT AFTER THAT
I'LL GO BACK TO BED

BUT I MUST GET THIS BILL PAID
OR SUFFER THAT DREADED LATE FEE
I CAN'T AFFORD THAT EXPENSE
WHAT'S GOING TO HAPPEN TO ME

I'LL JUST PUT HER ON SPEAKER
THEN I CAN DO MY OTHER STUFF
THEN AFTER ABOUT AN HOUR
I JUST DON'T HAVE ENOUGH

OH WELL, I'LL PUT MY TIME TO USE
AND WRITE THIS POEM WHILE I WAIT
AND HOPE SHE GETS BACK ON LINE
BEFORE SHE MAKES MY PAYMENT LATE

SIDE LINERS

by
Joseph Fram

OH! I KNOW YOU'VE SEEN THEM
SITTING THERE AND KNOWING ALL
THEY NEVER MISS A CHANCE
TO DISPUTE WHATEVER CALL

THEY ARE AT A BALL GAME
THEIR VOICES LOUD AND CLEAR
YOU MISS HALF THE ANNOUNCEMENTS
THEY MAKE SURE YOU CANNOT HEAR

THEN THEY ARE AT YOUR WORK
TELLING YOU THAT NOTHING'S RIGHT
THEY TRY TO RUIN ALL YOUR DAY
AND HOPE TO RUIN YOUR NIGHT

NO MATTER WHAT YOU DO OR SAY
SIDE LINERS HAVE TO HAVE A DIG
YOU THINK HOW SMALL AND PETTY
THEY THINK THEY ARE BIG

SIDE LINERS DON'T KNOW A THING
BUT THEY DON'T REALLY CARE
AS LONG AS THEY STIR THINGS UP
THEY ARE ALWAYS THERE

IT DOESN'T COUNT
by
Joseph Fram

LONG AGO WHEN I WAS YOUNG
WEIGHT WAS A PROBLEM THAT I HAD
I WOULD EAT EVERYTHING IN SIGHT
I GUESS I WAS REALLY BAD

I ATE AND I ATE, NEVER GETTING FULL
THEN I WOULD ASK FOR MORE
IF I HAD EATEN EVERYTHING
I WAS ONE UP ON THE SCORE

THEN ONE DAY IT HAPPENED
I FOUND MYSELF TOO FAT
WHEN I TRIED TO RUN UP A HILL
I WASN'T UP TO THAT

SO I FOUND A DIET
THAT WOULD SHED POUNDS GALORE
THE NIGHT I WAS TO START THE DIET
I THOUGHT "JUST ONE DONUT MORE"

"IT DOESN'T COUNT IN THE DARK"
SAID MY WIFE SWITCHING ON THE LIGHT
NOW I THANK HER FOR MY LOSS
I NEVER TOOK THAT FIRST BITE

CHECK PLEASE

by
Joseph Fram

"CHECK PLEASE" IS A SAYING
WHEN I WAS YOUNG WE HAD
AS A WAY TO LEAVE A SCENE
WE THOUGHT WAS GOING BAD

OR IT COULD BE LEGITIMATE
IN A DINER WHERE WE ATE
IF WE LINGERED MUCH TOO LONG
AND IT WAS GETTING LATE

I HEARD IT IN SOME PRODUCTIONS
AND PLAYS THAT I WOULD ATTEND
NOT TOO MUCH IN THE MIDDLE
MORE LIKELY AT THE END

I KINDA LIKE THAT SAYING
GETS ME OUT OF A SPOT
IN PLACES WHERE I AM
AND RATHER THAN I BE NOT

WHEN A SITUATION COMES ALONG
AND I WOULD LIKE TO LEAVE WITH EASE
I THINK ABOUT ALL THE TIMES
I EXCUSE MYSELF WITH "CHECK PLEASE"

HANDS FREE

by
Joseph Fram

THEY HAVE MADE LIFE SO EASY
WITH GADGETS GALORE
I THOUGHT WE HAVE ENOUGH
BUT THEY ARE MAKING MORE

WE HAVE HANDS FREE EVERYTHING
HANDS FREE TO ANSWER THE PHONE
THEY HAVE EVEN FOUND A WAY
FOR US NEVER TO BE ALONE

I SAW A HANDS FREE TELEVISION
YOU SAY A WORD AND IT IS ON
IT WILL EVEN TURN ITSELF OFF
IF IT THINKS THAT YOU ARE GONE

YOU HAVE BLU RAY PHONES
WHEN YOU GET INTO YOUR CAR
ANYONE CAN REACH YOU
IF YOU ARE NEAR OR FAR

BUT IT SCARED ME HALF TO DEATH
I KNEW THAT I HAD SEEN THE WORST
WHEN I SAW HANDS FREE DRIVING
HANDS FREE BECAME A CURSE

THAT'S WHY I'M HERE
by
Joseph Fram

I SUPPOSE YOU HAVE BEEN THERE
SITTING IN A DENTIST'S CHAIR
YOU THINK OF ALL THE PLACES
YOU'D RATHER BE THAN THERE

THEY START TO CLEAN YOUR TEETH
AND FILL YOUR MOUTH WITH STUFF
ASK YOU ALL KIND OF QUESTIONS
BUT YOU CAN'T SAY "THAT'S ENOUGH"

THEY ALWAYS SEEM TO FIND
PROBLEMS ON WHICH YOU DIDN'T COUNT
AND BECAUSE YOUR MOUTH IS FULL
YOU CAN'T OBJECT TO THE AMOUNT

THEN YOU GET A LECTURE
"YOU DON'T KNOW HOW TO FLOSS"
HOW ALL THAT PLAQUE IS GROWING
TO EXPLAIN THEY ARE AT A LOSS

WHEN THE LECTURE IS OVER
I TURN AND WHISPER IN HIS EAR
"THE PROBLEM IS I CAN'T GET IT
AND THAT'S WHY I AM HERE"

HELLO

by
Joseph Fram

A HOCKEY PLAYER I HAVE BEEN
FOR QUITE A LONG, LONG WHILE
I HAVE PLAYED MOSTLY FOR FUN
NOT NEAR YOUR PROFESSIONAL STYLE

WHEN I PLAYED MANY YEARS
NO CHEST PROTECTOR I WORE
I DON'T REMEMBER GETTING HIT
RARELY WAS I EVER SORE

ONE DAY THE TIME HAD COME
I WORE A PROTECTOR IN A GAME
I PUT IT ON, PAD AND JERSEY TOO
IT FELT PRETTY MUCH THE SAME

I SKATED IN A GAME THAT NIGHT
THEN I WAS BLIND SIDED HIT
I WAS KNOCKED DOWN ON THE ICE
MY SHOULDER GAVE ME QUITE A FIT

OUT ON THE ICE CAME AN EMT
AND PLACED BANDAGES ALL ABOUT
HE WRAPPED MY JERSEY PAD AND VEST
HELLO, HOW AM I SUPPOSED TO GET OUT

WHERE DID YOU GO
by
Joseph Fram

WHERE DID YOU GO MY SWEET DOREEN
YOU ARE GONE YET YOUR BODY IS HERE
THAT TERRIBLE DISEASE HAS TAKEN YOU
NOW WE LIVE IN CONSTANT FEAR

GONE IS THE PERSON I ONCE KNEW
SO ALIVE AND FULL OF FUN
I GUESS GOD HAS SENT HIS NOTE
THE LIFE YOU KNEW IS NOW DONE

DAYS AND NIGHTS BOTH THE SAME
YOU STRUGGLE TO DO SOME LITTLE THING
SIMPLE JOYS ESCAPE YOU NOW
THERE IS NO REASON FOR YOU TO SING

BUT I STILL SEE IN YOUR EYES
THAT LOVE FOR ME IS STILL THERE
AND AS LONG AS THERE IS A GLOW
I WON'T BE GOING ANYWHERE

FOR YOU ARE MY SWEET DOREEN
THE ONE I KNEW WHEN WE FIRST MET
AND NO MATTER WHERE YOU GO
THAT SWEET DOREEN I'LL NOT FORGET

TRAFFIC TICKET

by
Joseph Fram

YOU ARE DRIVING DOWN THE HIGHWAY
RANDOM THOUGHTS ARE IN YOUR HEAD
YOU'RE PUSHING ON THE GAS PEDAL
SHOULD BE PAYING ATTENTION INSTEAD

THEN YOU SEE THIS BLUE LIGHT
YOU KNOW YOU'RE NOT AT K-MART
IT GETS CLOSER IN YOUR REAR VIEW
BRINGS YOU BACK WITH QUITE A START

THEN A LARGE MAN IN BLUE
SAYS "ROLL YOUR WINDOW DOWN"
HOW DID HE GET THERE
I THOUGHT HE WAS IN TOWN

HE POLITELY ASKS YOU
FOR PAPERS IN YOUR CAR
YOU THINK HOW CAN I PUSH HIM
THEN YOU THINK NOT VERY FAR

ALL THOSE SMART ALECK ANSWERS
START RUNNING THROUGH YOUR HEAD
BUT THEN YOU WISELY CHANGE THEM
AND SAY "THANK YOU SIR" INSTEAD

LEARNING

by
Joseph Fram

TEACHING IS A TRICKY THING
TO GET SOMEONE TO LEARN
SEEMS THAT IS ONLY DONE
WHEN IT COMES THEIR TURN

OH, I KNOW WE LEARN A LOT
TAUGHT HOW TO READ AND WRITE
ALL THE FUNDAMENTALS
IN US TURNS ON A LIGHT

THEN AS WE GROW OLDER
WE LEARN A LOT IN SCHOOL
THEN WE TAKE WHAT WE WANT
AND MAKE THEM A USEFUL TOOL

BUT NOW HERE'S THE TRICKY PART
SO MUCH IS TAUGHT WE DON'T GET
EXCEPT FOR THINGS THAT INTEREST US
TEACHERS' EXPECTATIONS ARE NOT MET

I GUESS WE LEARN WHAT WE WANT
IN A WAY THAT PLEASES US
WE WILL DISREGARD OTHERS' PLANS
SO WHY PUT UP SUCH A FUSS

COLD CALLS

by
Joseph Fram

YOU ARE SITTING IN YOUR HOME
WATCHING YOUR FAVORITE GAME
SUDDENLY THE PHONE RINGS
SOMEONE GREETS YOU BY YOUR NAME

HELLO YOU TRY TO SAY
BUT BEFORE YOU CAN GET IT OUT
"I HAVE FOR YOU A LOVELY GIFT"
SOME COLD CALLER YOU HEAR SHOUT

"I AM IN THE MIDDLE OF MY GAME"
YOU TRY TO POLITELY SAY
YOU WOULD THINK THEY'D TAKE A HINT
THEY KEEP TALKING ANYWAY

WHEN YOU TELL THEM "NO THANK YOU"
THEY WANT ONE MOMENT MORE WITH YOU
YOU THINK YOU JUST CAN'T GET AWAY
BUT HERE IS ONE THING YOU CAN DO

PUT THE PHONE NEXT TO THE SPEAKER
AND GO ON AND ENJOY YOUR GAME
PERHAPS HE WILL NOT CALL AGAIN
IF YOU TREAT HIM JUST THE SAME

MONEY AND LOVE
by
Joseph Fram

MONEY AND LOVE
ARE JUST NOT THE SAME
WHEN YOU DON'T GET ENOUGH
YOU HAVE TO FIX A BLAME

WITH MONEY YOU COUNT
EVERY PENNY YOU EARN
HOW TO MAKE MORE
YOU QUICKLY CAN LEARN

LOVE IS A THING
THAT YOU GIVE AWAY
IF IT IS RETURNED
WITH YOU IT WILL STAY

IF YOU TRY TO HAVE BOTH
YOU ARE STUCK IN A BIND
IS IT MY MONEY OR THEIR LOVE
GOES THROUGH YOUR MIND

THERE IS NEVER ENOUGH MONEY
FOR THOSE WHO SEEK SUCH
THERE IS ALWAYS ENOUGH LOVE
FOR THE LIVES YOU TOUCH

LIGHT A BURNT MATCH

by
Joseph Fram

A BURNED OUT MATCH CANNOT BE STRUCK
NO MATTER HOW HARD YOU MAY TRY
IT HAS DONE WHAT IT SUPPOSED TO DO
THERE IS NO OTHER REASON WHY

SOMETIMES YOU ARE IN A SITUATION
WHERE YOU TRY TO GIVE A LITTLE MORE
BUT YOUR BODY CANNOT TAKE IT
ALL YOU WIND UP IS BEING SORE

OTHERS MAY TRY TO PUSH YOU
TO DO THINGS BEYOND YOUR SKILL
AND YOU KNOW RIGHT FROM THE START
CAN'T NOW AND NEVER WILL

THERE ARE TIMES IN YOUR LIFE
YOU CAN SEE WHERE YOU ARE LOST
BECAUSE YOU ARE A BURNT MATCH
YOU HAVE TO PAY THE COST

I LIKEN A BURNED OUT MATCH
TO THINGS IN MY LIFE PLAN
DOING WHAT I'M SUPPOSED TO DO
AND THAT'S ABOUT ALL I CAN

MY MEMORIES
by
Joseph Fram

MEMORIES BUILT UPON A LIFETIME
ARE STORED SOMEWHERE IN MY MIND
OF HAPPY TIMES AND GREATER GLORY
AND OTHER THINGS THAT I CAN FIND

MY FONDEST ONES WHEN I WAS YOUNG
ARE OF MY CHILDREN AND MY WIFE
OH! HOW I TRIED TO SHOW TO THEM
THEY WERE THE CENTER OF MY LIFE

OTHER THINGS I HAD TO DO
TO KEEP THIS FAMILY INTACT
SOME MISTAKES THAT I HAD MADE
YES, I WISH I HAD THEM BACK

THEN THOSE MEMORIES FADE AWAY
FOR THEY ARE THERE NO MORE
ALL I HAD TO HOLD ON TO
WENT AWAY AND CLOSED THE DOOR

WHERE DO I PUT THOSE MEMORIES
WHEN GONE ARE THOSE THAT SHARED
MY MEMORIES LIE IN WASTE
LIKE MY LOVE I THOUGHT HAD CARED

SPELL CHECK

by
Joseph Fram

I USED TO KEEP A DICTIONARY
CLOSE BY WHEN I WRITE
TO COMPOSE A SIMPLE LETTER
SOMETIMES TURNED INTO A FIGHT

I KNEW WHAT I WANTED TO SAY
BUT TO SPELL IT WAS ALL WRONG
LOOKING UP EVERY OTHER WORD
MADE MY WRITING VERY LONG

SOMETIMES I WOULD GET STUCK
DIDN'T KNOW LETTERS IN THE WORD
IF I ASKED THOSE AROUND ME
SOMETHING THEY HAD NEVER HEARD

THEN I GOT THIS COMPUTER
I AM NOW HAPPY AS CAN BE
WHEN I AM TYPING SOMETHING
IT DOES THE WORK FOR ME

FOR I DISCOVERED SPELL CHECK
THE LITTLE RED CHECK UP ABOVE
I FINISH THINGS IN HALF THE TIME
IT IS SOMETHING I JUST LOVE

AH! COMFORT

by
Joseph Fram

ONE FINE SUNDAY MORN
ON A GOLF DRIVING RANGE
I WAS HITTING SOME BALLS
WHEN I SAW SOMETHING STRANGE

RIGHT NEXT TO ME
A PRO WAS HAVING A FIT
TEACHING A NEW PLAYER
HOW HE SHOULD HIT

HE PLACED HIS HANDS ON THE CLUB
THE POSITION HE WANTED WAS RIGHT
TOLD THE STUDENT TO SWING
AND WATCHED THE BALL'S FLIGHT

HE WENT AWAY FOR A WHILE
THE STUDENT REVERTED HIS STANCE
THE PRO KNEW THAT HE DID
WITH JUST A SMALL GLANCE

"WHAT YOU TOLD ME TO DO
IS NOT COMFORTABLE FOR ME"
"IF IT'S COMFORT YOU WANT
IN THE BAR YOU SHOULD BE"

GOD IS ON MY SIDE
by
Joseph Fram

LIKE ALL, I HAVE MY UPS AND DOWNS
SOMETIMES THE DOWNS ARE CRUEL
I WIND UP ON THE SHORT SIDE
OTHERS DON'T FOLLOW THE GOLDEN RULE

BUT I HAVE LEARNED THE HARD WAY
THERE IS A REASON FOR EVERYTHING
WHEN I CAN'T HEAR MY MUSIC
GOD SENDS THE BIRDS TO SING

WHEN I DO NOT GET MY WAY
I LOOK FOR THE REASON WHY
GOD HAS TAKEN AWAY A TASK
SO ANOTHER I CAN TRY

IS IT A CURSE OR A BLESSING
WHEN AN OBSTACLE IS PUT IN MY WAY
GOD SHOWS US MANY PATHS
HE CHOOSES ON THE ONE WE STAY

IN ALL THE TRIALS IN LIFE I FACE
I KNOW THAT GOD IS ON MY SIDE
SO I KEEP AN OPEN BOOK
I NEVER HAVE ANYTHING TO HIDE

WON'T KNOW TILL IT'S OVER
by
Joseph Fram

I KNOW WE ALL HAVE DONE THIS
SUFFERED FROM BUYER'S REGRET
IT COMES FROM BUYING SOMETHING
YOUR EXPECTATIONS WERE NOT MET

OR YOU JUST MEET SOMEONE
YOU THINK WILL CHANGE YOUR LIFE
YOU GIVE YOUR HEART AND SOUL
YOU THINK SHE WILL BE YOUR WIFE

THEN THERE IS THE BUSINESS DEAL
YOU WORK SO HARD TO ACQUIRE
ONCE YOU GET IT RUNNING GOOD
YOU CAN'T WAIT TILL YOU RETIRE

WE MAKE CHOICES ALL THE TIME
MOST ARE DONE WITH EASE
SOME ARE HARD TO LIVE WITH
OTHERS WE CAN NEVER PLEASE

I WON'T KNOW TILL IT'S OVER
IF MY CHOICE WAS RIGHT OR WRONG
MY LIFE IS FILLED WITH QUESTIONS
I STILL ASK WHERE I BELONG

Have you read Joseph's Journey
Volumes 1, 2, 3, 4 & 5?

- - - - - - - - - - - -

Joseph's Journey, Volume 1
Poetry of Hope, Help, Healing and Humor

Joseph's Journey, Volume 2
Psychological Concepts Expressed in Poetry

Joseph's Journey, Volume 3
A Look at the Flip Side of My Life

Joseph's Journey, Volume 4
A Look in My Rear View Mirror:
"Did I just Waste a Precious Life –
That Kept Mine from Being Used"

Joseph's Journey, Volume 5
Parkinson's up-close:
Life changing events that only
you and God can reconcile

Copies of these and other books can be ordered by sending the name of the book(s) and your name and address with a check or money order for $7.95 + $2.95 shipping & handling (total = $10.90 per book) made payable to:

Everlasting Publishing
P.O. Box 965
Vancouver, WA 98666-0965
USA

Also available to purchase online:
everlastingpublishing.org